MEL BAY'S

GUITAR JOURNALS

MASTERING THE FINGERBOARD
THE READING BOOK

1 2 3 4 5 6 7 8 9 0

Visit us on the Web at www.melbay.com — E-mail us at email@melbay.com

CONTENTS

STRING STUDIES 3

NOTE STUDIES 6

KEY OF C 8

KEY OF A MINOR 12

KEY OF G 16

KEY OF E MINOR 20

KEY OF D 24

KEY OF B MINOR 28

KEY OF A 32

KEY OF F SHARP MINOR 36

KEY OF E 40

KEY OF C SHARP MINOR 44

KEY OF B 48

KEY OF G SHARP MINOR 52

KEY OF F 56

KEY OF D MINOR 60

KEY OF B FLAT 64

KEY OF G MINOR 68

KEY OF E FLAT 72

KEY OF C MINOR 76

KEY OF A FLAT 80

KEY OF F MINOR 84

KEY OF D FLAT 88

KEY OF B FLAT MINOR 92

KEY OF G FLAT 96

KEY OF E FLAT MINOR 100

KEY REVIEWS 104

My idea in writing this book was to create great playing material which would accomplish a number of goals. First it would present a collection of wonderful music, very guitaristic in sound, suitable for study or performance. Next, it would create a body of musical literature designed to specifically impart mastery of the fingerboard and facility in playing in all positions and all keys. The book starts with single string studies and moves on to same note studies. The actual etudes begin on page 8. There are four etudes presented for each key, each one being in a different position on the fingerboard. The etudes are not to be phrased in a jazz or swing style. They are to be interpreted in a classical manner, similar to a Bach invention. I encourage you to use a maximum of expression and rhythmic flexibility in the performance of these etudes. These etudes also are a wonderful vehicle for developing attack and tone on the instrument. Feel free to use and vary subtle nuances in terms of picking styles and dynamics. The final section of the book starting on page 104 presents comprehensive reviews for each key. An etude is presented which starts in a lower position and moves progressively up the fingerboard. This etude should be played as one complete piece of music. Finally, I would like to point out that the etudes in this book have been written around a prescribed position on the guitar; however there are some cases where the position must be broken to play a certain passage or line. In these cases, refer to the fingerings in the book or find logical fingerings that are comfortable to you.

My hope is that this book will be a treasured collection of music which will on a daily and weekly basis provide meaningful avenues of expression.

NOTES ON THE FIRST STRING

FIRST STRING STUDY

PLAY ALL NOTES ON THE FIRST STRING

NOTES ON THE SECOND STRING

SECOND STRING STUDY

PLAY ALL NOTES ON THE SECOND STRING

NOTES ON THE THIRD STRING

THIRD STRING STUDY

PLAY ALL NOTES ON THE THIRD STRING

NOTES ON THE FOURTH STRING

FOURTH STRING STUDY

PLAY ALL NOTES ON THE FOURTH STRING

NOTES ON THE FIFTH STRING

FIFTH STRING STUDY

PLAY ALL NOTES ON THE FIFTH STRING

NOTES ON THE SIXTH STRING

SIXTH STRING STUDY

PLAY ALL NOTES ON THE SIXTH STRING

6

KEY OF C

C SCALE - OPEN POSITION

C ARPEGGIO - OPEN POSITION

C STUDY #1 - OPEN POSITION

Fine

D.C. al Fine

KEY OF C

C SCALE - 2ND POSITION

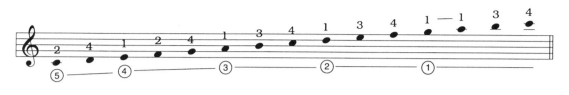

C ARPEGGIO - 2ND POSITION

C STUDY #2 - 2ND POSITION

(PLAY NO OPEN STRING NOTES)

KEY OF C

C SCALE - 5TH POSITION

C ARPEGGIO - 5TH POSITION

C STUDY #3 - 5TH POSITION

10

KEY OF C

C SCALE - 7TH POSITION

C ARPEGGIO - 7TH POSITION

C STUDY #4 - 7TH POSITION

KEY OF A MINOR

A MINOR SCALE / HARMONIC MODE - OPEN POSITION

A MINOR ARPEGGIO - OPEN POSITION

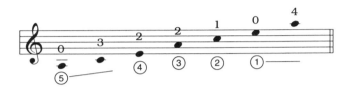

A MINOR STUDY #1 - OPEN POSITION

Fine

D.C. al Fine

KEY OF A MINOR

A MINOR SCALE / HARMONIC MODE - 2ND POSITION

A MINOR ARPEGGIO - 2ND POSITION

A MINOR STUDY #2 - 2ND POSITION

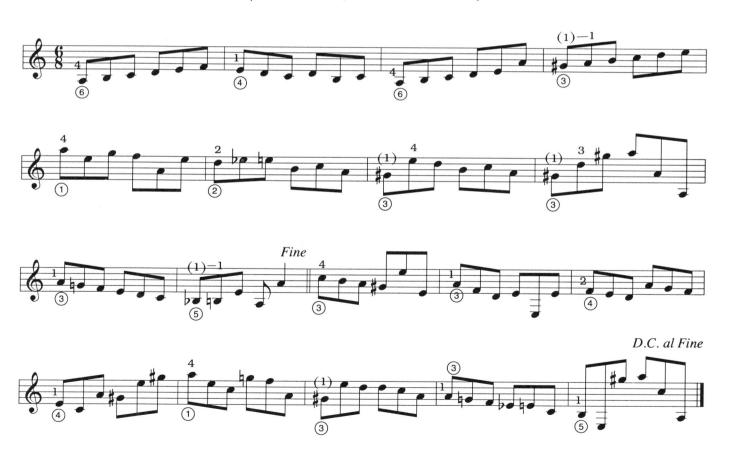

KEY OF A MINOR

A MINOR SCALE / HARMONIC MODE - 5TH POSITION

A MINOR ARPEGGIO - 5TH POSITION

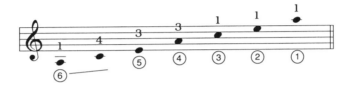

A MINOR STUDY #3 - 5TH POSITION

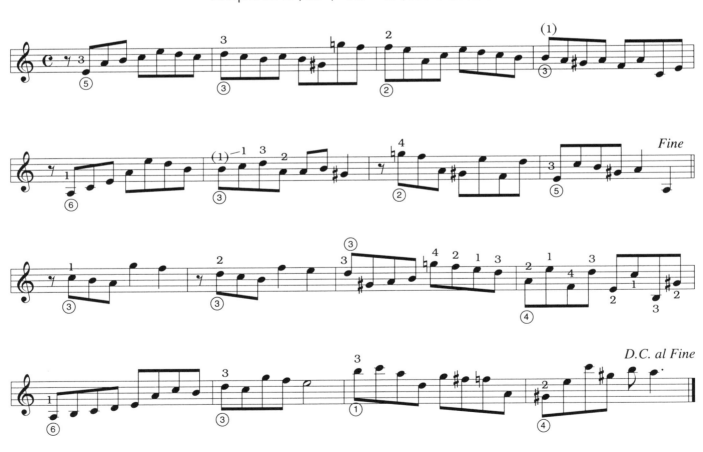

KEY OF A MINOR

A MINOR SCALE / HARMONIC MODE - 9TH POSITION

A MINOR ARPEGGIO - 9TH POSITION

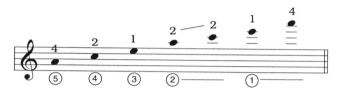

A MINOR STUDY #4 - 9TH POSITION

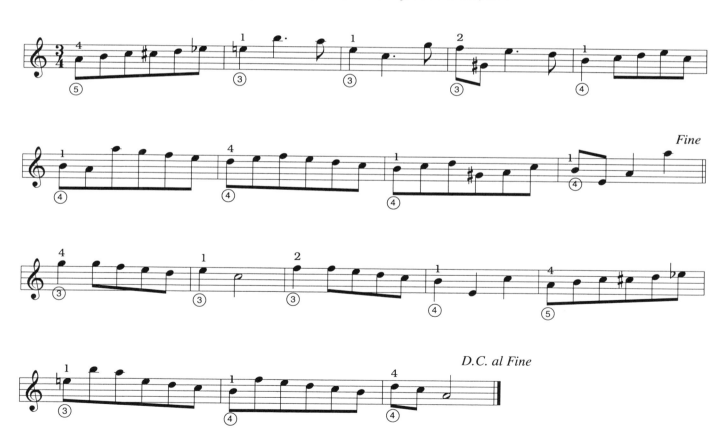

15

KEY OF G

G SCALE - OPEN POSITION

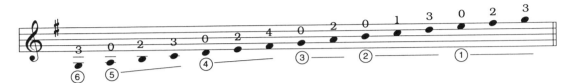

G ARPEGGIO - OPEN POSITION

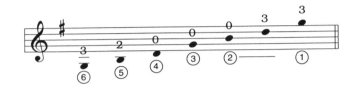

G STUDY #1 - OPEN POSITION

KEY OF G

G SCALE - 2ND POSITION

G ARPEGGIO - 2ND POSITION

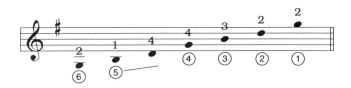

G STUDY #2 - 2ND POSITION

KEY OF G

G SCALE - 7TH POSITION [C LYDIAN]

G ARPEGGIO - 7TH POSITION

G STUDY #3 - 7TH POSITION

KEY OF G

G SCALE - 9TH POSITION [D MIXO]

G ARPEGGIO - 9TH POSITION

G STUDY #4 - 9TH POSITION

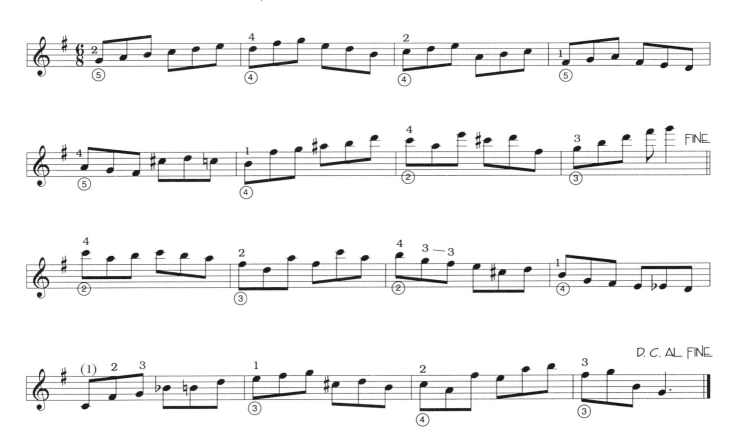

KEY OF E MINOR

E MINOR SCALE / HARMONIC MODE - OPEN POSITION

E MINOR ARPEGGIO - OPEN POSITION

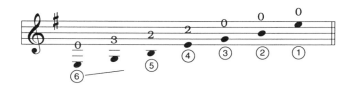

E MINOR STUDY #1 - OPEN POSITION

20

KEY OF E MINOR

E MINOR SCALE / HARMONIC MODE - 4TH POSITION

E MINOR ARPEGGIO - 4TH POSITION

E MINOR STUDY #2 - 4TH POSITION

KEY OF E MINOR

E MINOR SCALE / HARMONIC MODE - 7TH POSITION

E MINOR ARPEGGIO - 7TH POSITION

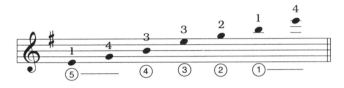

E MINOR STUDY #3 - 7TH POSITION

22

KEY OF E MINOR

E MINOR SCALE / HARMONIC MODE - 9TH POSITION

E MINOR ARPEGGIO - 9TH POSITION

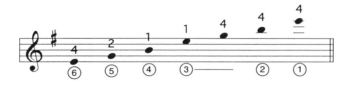

E MINOR STUDY #4 - 9TH POSITION

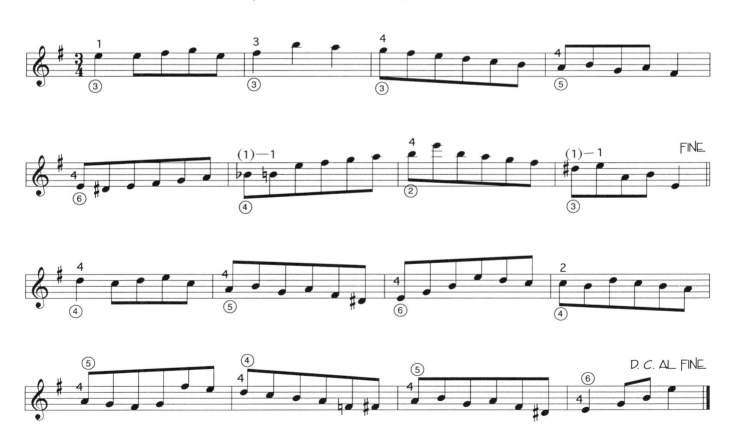

KEY OF D

D SCALE - 2ND POSITION

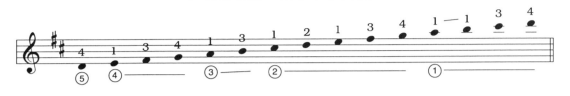

D ARPEGGIO - 2ND POSITION

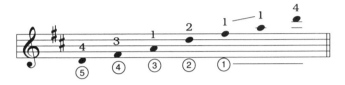

D STUDY #1 - 2ND POSITION

KEY OF D

D SCALE - 4TH POSITION

D ARPEGGIO - 4TH POSITION

D STUDY #2 - 4TH POSITION

25

KEY OF D

D SCALE - 7TH POSITION

D ARPEGGIO - 7TH POSITION

D STUDY #3 - 7TH POSITION

KEY OF D

D SCALE - 9TH POSITION

D ARPEGGIO - 9TH POSITION

D STUDY #4 - 9TH POSITION

KEY OF B MINOR

B MINOR SCALE / HARMONIC MODE - 2ND POSITION

B MINOR ARPEGGIO - 2ND POSITION

B MINOR STUDY #1 - 2ND POSITION

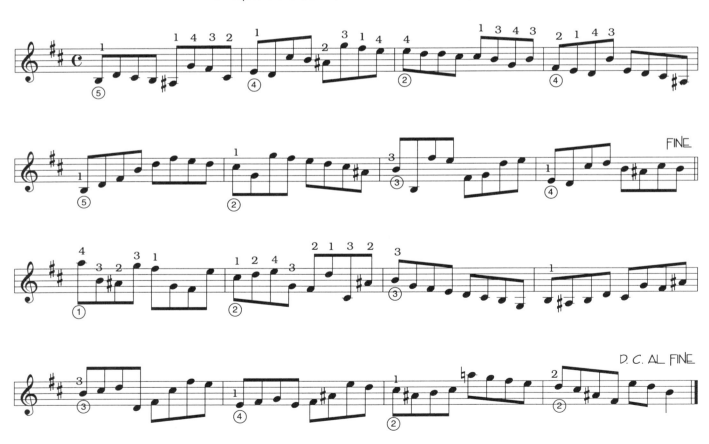

KEY OF B MINOR

B MINOR SCALE / HARMONIC MODE - 4TH POSITION

B MINOR ARPEGGIO - 4TH POSITION

B MINOR STUDY #2 - 4TH POSITION

KEY OF B MINOR

B MINOR SCALE / HARMONIC MODE - 7TH POSITION

B MINOR ARPEGGIO - 7TH POSITION

B MINOR STUDY #3 - 7TH POSITION

KEY OF B MINOR

B MINOR SCALE / HARMONIC MODE - 11TH POSITION

B MINOR ARPEGGIO - 11TH POSITION

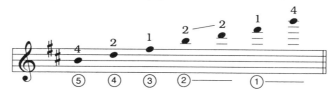

B MINOR STUDY #4 - 11TH POSITION

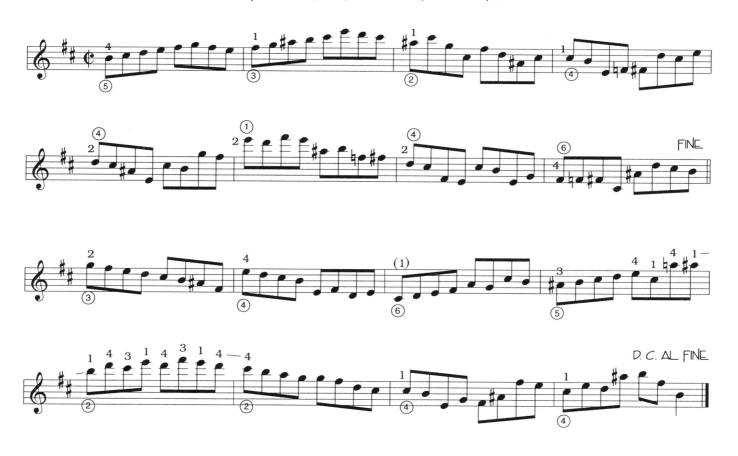

KEY OF A

A SCALE - OPEN POSITION

A ARPEGGIO - OPEN POSITION

A STUDY #1 - OPEN POSITION

FINE

D. C. AL FINE

KEY OF A

A SCALE - 2ND POSITION

A ARPEGGIO - 2ND POSITION

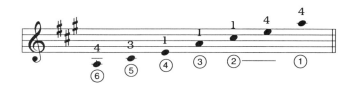

A STUDY #2 - 2ND POSITION

KEY OF A

A SCALE - 4TH POSITION

A ARPEGGIO - 4TH POSITION

A STUDY #3 - 4TH POSITION

KEY OF A

A SCALE - 9TH POSITION

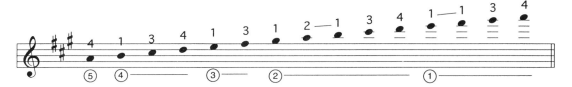

A ARPEGGIO - 9TH POSITION

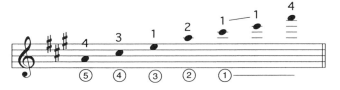

A STUDY #4 - 9TH POSITION

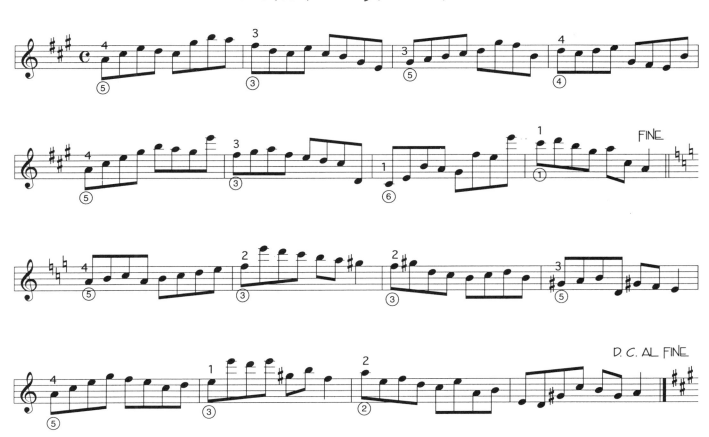

KEY OF F SHARP MINOR

F SHARP MINOR SCALE / HARMONIC MODE - 2ND POSITION

F SHARP MINOR ARPEGGIO - 2ND POSITION

F SHARP MINOR STUDY #1 - 2ND POSITION

KEY OF F SHARP MINOR

F SHARP MINOR SCALE / HARMONIC MODE - 6TH POSITION

F SHARP MINOR ARPEGGIO - 6TH POSITION

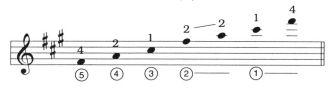

F SHARP MINOR STUDY #2 - 6TH POSITION

KEY OF F SHARP MINOR

F SHARP MINOR SCALE / HARMONIC MODE - 9TH POSITION

F SHARP MINOR ARPEGGIO - 9TH POSITION

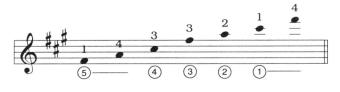

F SHARP MINOR STUDY #3 - 9TH POSITION

KEY OF F SHARP MINOR

F SHARP MINOR SCALE / HARMONIC MODE - 11TH POSITION

F SHARP MINOR ARPEGGIO - 11TH POSITION

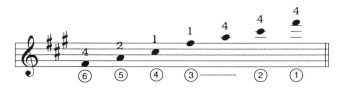

F SHARP MINOR STUDY #4 - 11TH POSITION

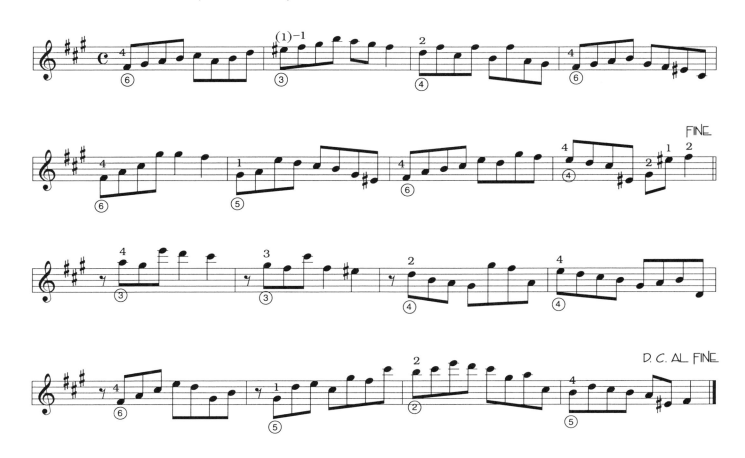

KEY OF E

E SCALE - OPEN POSITION

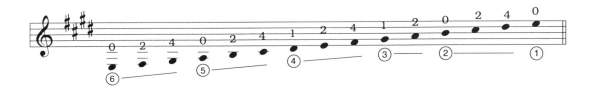

E ARPEGGIO - OPEN POSITION

E STUDY #1 - OPEN POSITION

40

KEY OF E

E SCALE - 4TH POSITION

E ARPEGGIO - 4TH POSITION

E STUDY #2 - 4TH POSITION

KEY OF E

E SCALE - 6TH POSITION

E ARPEGGIO - 6TH POSITION

E STUDY #3 - 6TH POSITION

42

KEY OF E

E SCALE - 9TH POSITION

E ARPEGGIO - 9TH POSITION

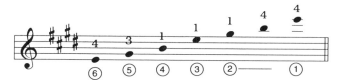

E STUDY #4 - 9TH POSITION

43

KEY OF C SHARP MINOR

C SHARP MINOR SCALE / HARMONIC MODE - 1ST POSITION

C SHARP MINOR ARPEGGIO - 1ST POSITION

C SHARP MINOR STUDY #1 - 1ST POSITION

KEY OF C SHARP MINOR

C SHARP MINOR SCALE / HARMONIC MODE - 4TH POSITION

C SHARP MINOR ARPEGGIO - 4TH POSITION

C SHARP MINOR STUDY #2 - 4TH POSITION

KEY OF C SHARP MINOR

C SHARP MINOR SCALE / HARMONIC MODE - 6TH POSITION

C SHARP MINOR ARPEGGIO - 6TH POSITION

C SHARP MINOR STUDY #3 - 6TH POSITION

KEY OF C SHARP MINOR

C SHARP MINOR SCALE / HARMONIC MODE - 9TH POSITION

C SHARP MINOR ARPEGGIO - 9TH POSITION

C SHARP MINOR STUDY #4 - 9TH POSITION

47

KEY OF B

B SCALE - 1ST POSITION

B ARPEGGIO - 1ST POSITION

B STUDY #1 - 1ST POSITION

KEY OF B

B SCALE - 4TH POSITION

B ARPEGGIO - 4TH POSITION

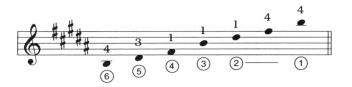

B STUDY #2 - 4TH POSITION

KEY OF B

B SCALE - 6TH POSITION

B ARPEGGIO - 6TH POSITION

B STUDY #3 - 6TH POSITION

KEY OF B

B SCALE - 11TH POSITION

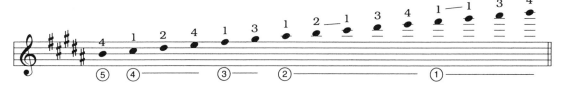

B ARPEGGIO - 11TH POSITION

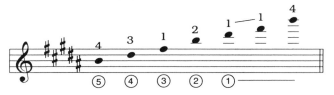

B STUDY #4 - 11TH POSITION

KEY OF G SHARP MINOR

G SHARP MINOR SCALE / HARMONIC MODE - 1ST POSITION

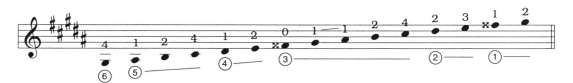

G SHARP MINOR ARPEGGIO - 1ST POSITION

G SHARP MINOR STUDY #1 - 1ST POSITION

KEY OF G SHARP MINOR

G SHARP MINOR SCALE / HARMONIC MODE - 4TH POSITION

G SHARP MINOR ARPEGGIO - 4TH POSITION

G SHARP MINOR STUDY #2 - 4TH POSITION

KEY OF G SHARP MINOR

G SHARP MINOR SCALE / HARMONIC MODE - 8TH POSITION

G SHARP MINOR ARPEGGIO - 8TH POSITION

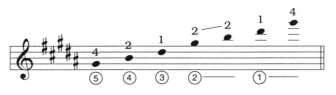

G SHARP MINOR STUDY #3 - 8TH POSITION

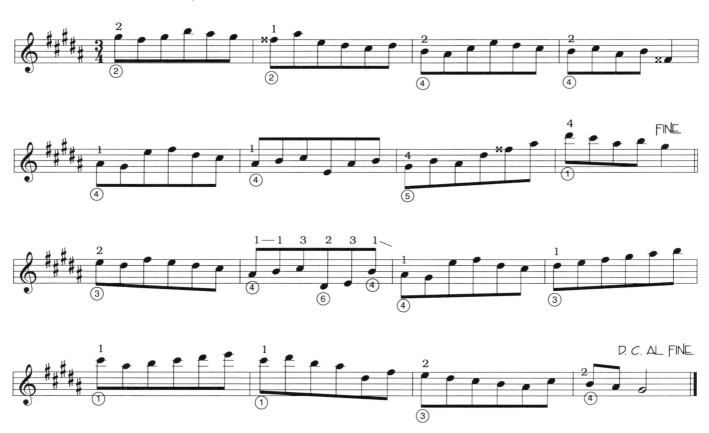

KEY OF G SHARP MINOR

G SHARP MINOR SCALE / HARMONIC MODE - 11TH POSITION

G SHARP MINOR ARPEGGIO - 11TH POSITION

G SHARP MINOR STUDY #4 - 11TH POSITION

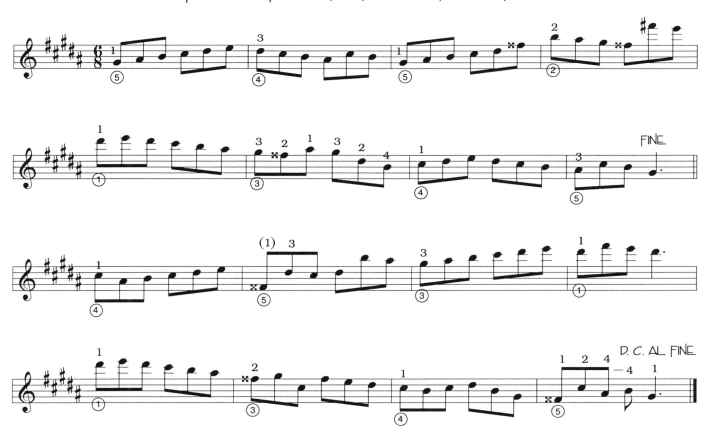

KEY OF F

F SCALE - OPEN POSITION

F ARPEGGIO - OPEN POSITION

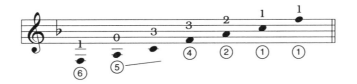

F STUDY #1 - OPEN POSITION

KEY OF F

F SCALE - 5TH POSITION

F ARPEGGIO - 5TH POSITION

F STUDY #2 - 5TH POSITION

KEY OF F

F SCALE - 7TH POSITION

F ARPEGGIO - 7TH POSITION

F STUDY #3 - 7TH POSITION

KEY OF F

F SCALE - 10TH POSITION

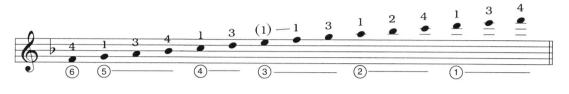

F ARPEGGIO - 10TH POSITION

F STUDY #4 - 10TH POSITION

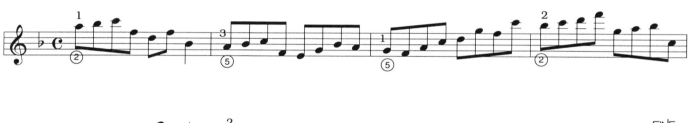

KEY OF D MINOR

D MINOR SCALE / HARMONIC MODE - 2ND POSITION

D MINOR ARPEGGIO - 2ND POSITION

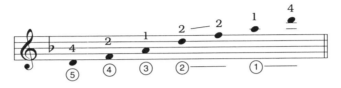

D MINOR STUDY #1 - 2ND POSITION

60

KEY OF D MINOR

D MINOR SCALE / HARMONIC MODE - 5TH POSITION

D MINOR ARPEGGIO - 5TH POSITION

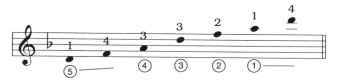

D MINOR STUDY #2 - 5TH POSITION

KEY OF D MINOR

D MINOR SCALE / HARMONIC MODE - 7TH POSITION

D MINOR ARPEGGIO - 7TH POSITION

D MINOR STUDY #3 - 7TH POSITION

KEY OF D MINOR

D MINOR SCALE / HARMONIC MODE - 10TH POSITION

D MINOR ARPEGGIO - 10TH POSITION

D MINOR STUDY #4 - 10TH POSITION

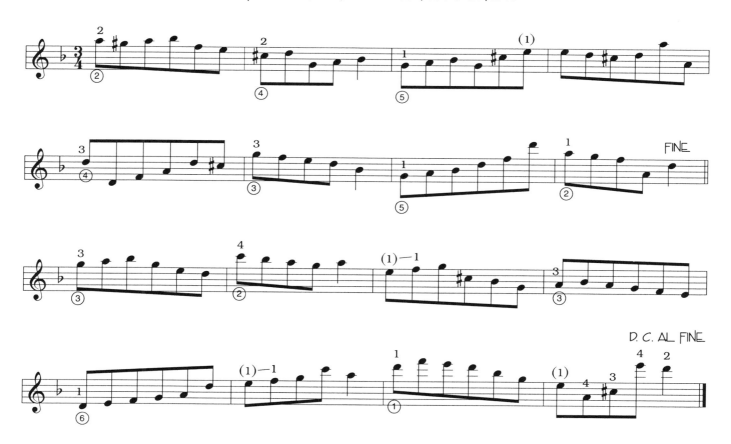

KEY OF B FLAT

B FLAT SCALE - OPEN POSITION

B FLAT ARPEGGIO - OPEN POSITION

B FLAT STUDY #1 - OPEN POSITION

KEY OF B FLAT

B FLAT SCALE - 3RD POSITION

B FLAT ARPEGGIO - 3RD POSITION

B FLAT STUDY #2 - 3RD POSITION

65

KEY OF B FLAT

B FLAT SCALE - 5TH POSITION

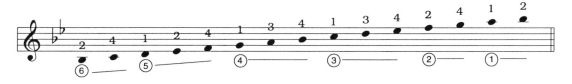

B FLAT ARPEGGIO - 5TH POSITION

B FLAT STUDY #3 - 5TH POSITION

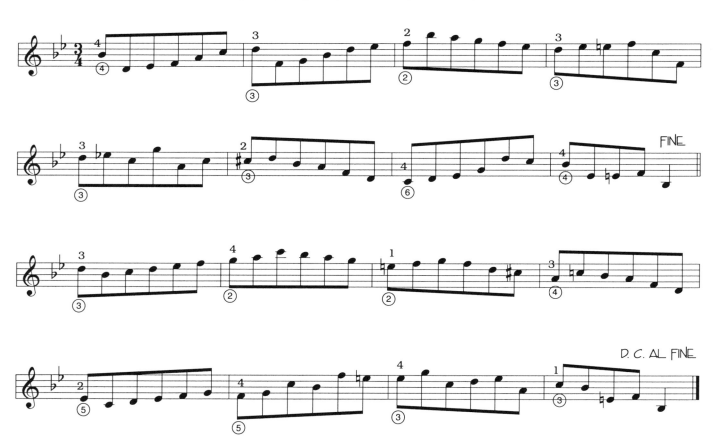

KEY OF B FLAT

B FLAT SCALE - 10TH POSITION

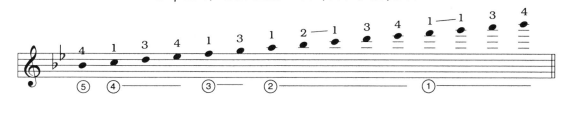

B FLAT ARPEGGIO - 10TH POSITION

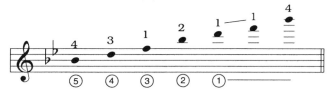

B FLAT STUDY #4 - 10TH POSITION

KEY OF G MINOR

G MINOR SCALE / HARMONIC MODE - OPEN POSITION

G MINOR ARPEGGIO - OPEN POSITION

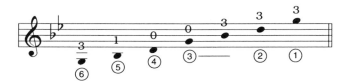

G MINOR STUDY #1 - OPEN POSITION

KEY OF G MINOR

G MINOR SCALE / HARMONIC MODE - 3RD POSITION

G MINOR ARPEGGIO - 3RD POSITION

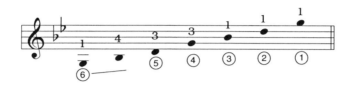

G MINOR STUDY #2 - 3RD POSITION

KEY OF G MINOR

G MINOR SCALE / HARMONIC MODE - 7TH POSITION

G MINOR ARPEGGIO - 7TH POSITION

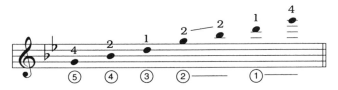

G MINOR STUDY #3 - 7TH POSITION

KEY OF G MINOR

G MINOR SCALE / HARMONIC MODE - 10TH POSITION

G MINOR ARPEGGIO - 10TH POSITION

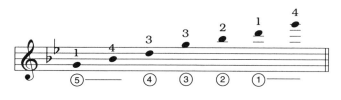

G MINOR STUDY #4 - 10TH POSITION

KEY OF E FLAT

E FLAT SCALE - 3RD POSITION

E FLAT ARPEGGIO - 3RD POSITION

E FLAT STUDY #1 - 3RD POSITION

KEY OF E FLAT

E FLAT SCALE - 5TH POSITION

E FLAT ARPEGGIO - 5TH POSITION

E FLAT STUDY #2 - 5TH POSITION

KEY OF E FLAT

E FLAT SCALE - 8TH POSITION

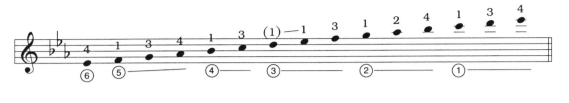

E FLAT ARPEGGIO - 8TH POSITION

E FLAT STUDY #3 - 8TH POSITION

KEY OF E FLAT

E FLAT SCALE - 10TH POSITION

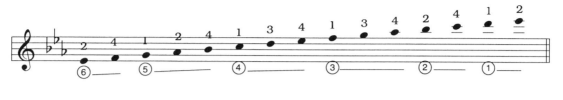

E FLAT ARPEGGIO - 10TH POSITION

E FLAT STUDY #4 - 10TH POSITION

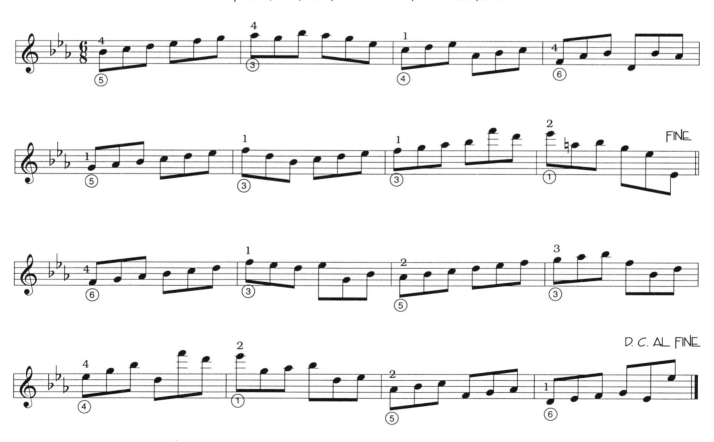

KEY OF C MINOR

C MINOR SCALE / HARMONIC MODE - OPEN POSITION

C MINOR ARPEGGIO - OPEN POSITION

C MINOR STUDY #1 - OPEN POSITION

FINE

D. C. AL FINE

KEY OF C MINOR

C MINOR SCALE / HARMONIC MODE - 3RD POSITION

C MINOR ARPEGGIO - 3RD POSITION

C MINOR STUDY #2 - 3RD POSITION

KEY OF C MINOR

C MINOR SCALE / HARMONIC MODE - 5TH POSITION

C MINOR ARPEGGIO - 5TH POSITION

C MINOR STUDY #3 - 5TH POSITION

KEY OF C MINOR

C MINOR SCALE / HARMONIC MODE - 8TH POSITION

C MINOR ARPEGGIO - 8TH POSITION

C MINOR STUDY #4 - 8TH POSITION

KEY OF A FLAT

A FLAT SCALE - OPEN POSITION

A FLAT ARPEGGIO - OPEN POSITION

A FLAT STUDY #1 - OPEN POSITION

KEY OF A FLAT

A FLAT SCALE - 3RD POSITION

A FLAT ARPEGGIO - 3RD POSITION

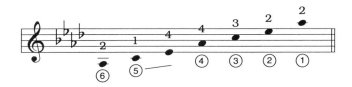

A FLAT STUDY #2 - 3RD POSITION

KEY OF A FLAT

A FLAT SCALE - 8TH POSITION

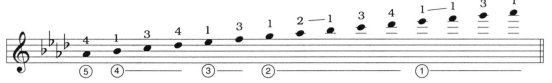

A FLAT ARPEGGIO - 8TH POSITION

A FLAT STUDY #3 - 8TH POSITION

KEY OF A FLAT

A FLAT SCALE - 10TH POSITION

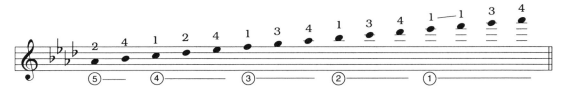

A FLAT ARPEGGIO - 10TH POSITION

A FLAT STUDY #4 - 10TH POSITION

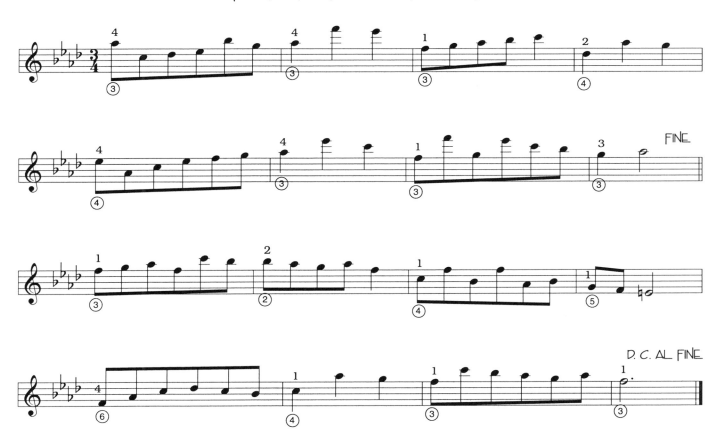

KEY OF F MINOR

F MINOR SCALE / HARMONIC MODE – 1ST POSITION

F MINOR ARPEGGIO – 1ST POSITION

F MINOR STUDY #1 – 1ST POSITION

84

KEY OF F MINOR

F MINOR SCALE / HARMONIC MODE - 5TH POSITION

F MINOR ARPEGGIO - 5TH POSITION

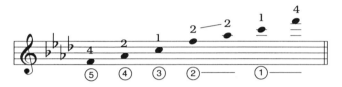

F MINOR STUDY #2 - 5TH POSITION

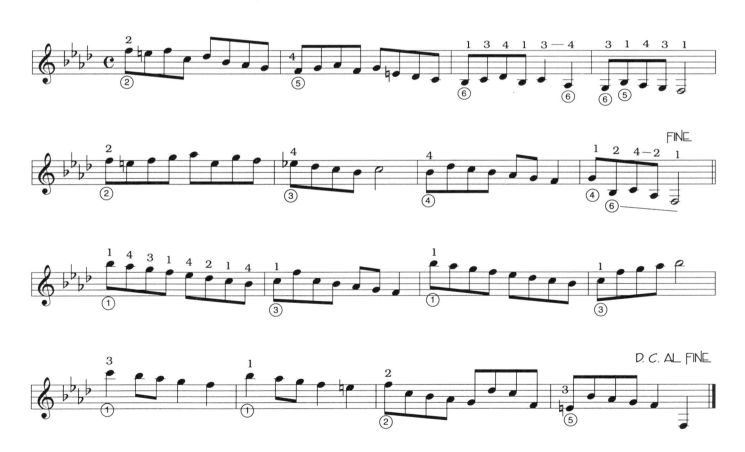

KEY OF F MINOR

F MINOR SCALE / HARMONIC MODE - 8TH POSITION

F MINOR ARPEGGIO - 8TH POSITION

F MINOR STUDY #3 - 8TH POSITION

KEY OF F MINOR

F MINOR SCALE / HARMONIC MODE - 10TH POSITION

F MINOR ARPEGGIO - 10TH POSITION

F MINOR STUDY #4 - 10TH POSITION

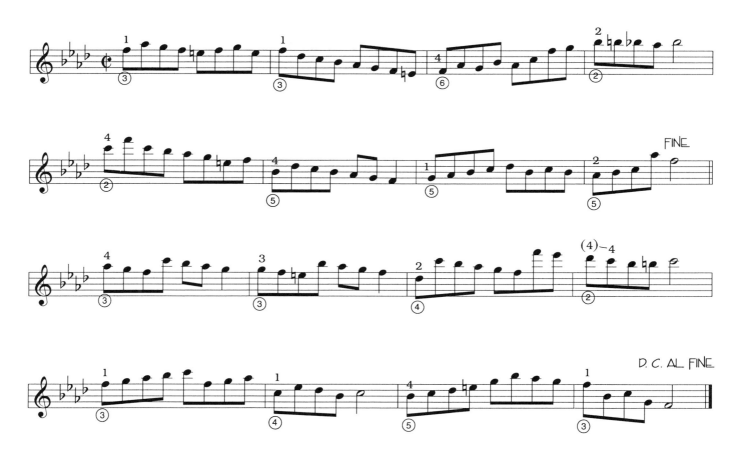

KEY OF D FLAT

D FLAT SCALE - 1ST POSITION

D FLAT ARPEGGIO - 1ST POSITION

D FLAT STUDY #1 - 1ST POSITION

KEY OF D FLAT

D FLAT SCALE - 3RD POSITION

D FLAT ARPEGGIO - 3RD POSITION

D FLAT STUDY #2 - 3RD POSITION

89

KEY OF D FLAT

D FLAT SCALE - 6TH POSITION

D FLAT ARPEGGIO - 6TH POSITION

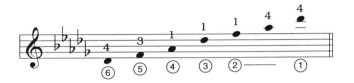

D FLAT STUDY #3 - 6TH POSITION

KEY OF D FLAT

D FLAT SCALE - 8TH POSITION

D FLAT ARPEGGIO - 8TH POSITION

D FLAT STUDY #4 - 8TH POSITION

91

KEY OF B FLAT MINOR

B FLAT MINOR SCALE / HARMONIC MODE - 1ST POSITION

B FLAT MINOR ARPEGGIO - 1ST POSITION

B FLAT MINOR STUDY #1 - 1ST POSITION

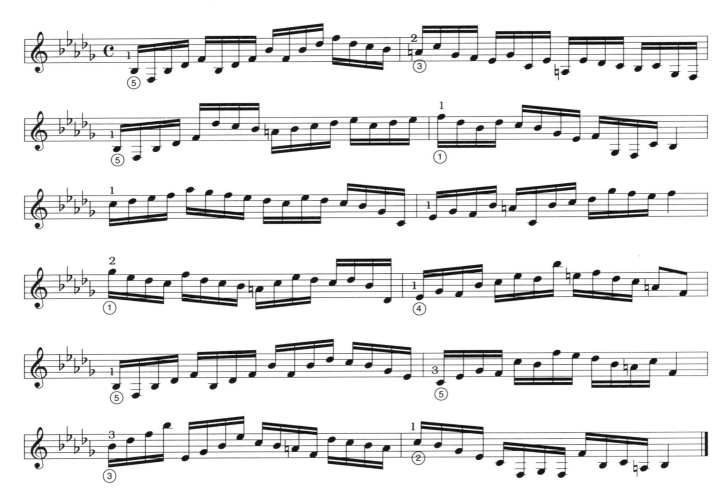

KEY OF B FLAT MINOR

B FLAT MINOR SCALE / HARMONIC MODE - 3RD POSITION

B FLAT MINOR ARPEGGIO - 3RD POSITION

B FLAT MINOR STUDY #2 - 3RD POSITION

KEY OF B FLAT MINOR

B FLAT MINOR SCALE / HARMONIC MODE - 6TH POSITION

B FLAT MINOR ARPEGGIO - 6TH POSITION

B FLAT MINOR STUDY #3 - 6TH POSITION

KEY OF B FLAT MINOR

B FLAT MINOR SCALE / HARMONIC MODE - 10TH POSITION

B FLAT MINOR ARPEGGIO - 10TH POSITION

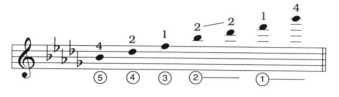

B FLAT MINOR STUDY #4 - 10TH POSITION

KEY OF G FLAT

G FLAT SCALE - 1ST POSITION

G FLAT ARPEGGIO - 1ST POSITION

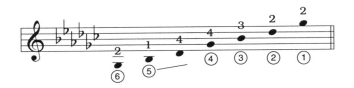

G FLAT STUDY #1 - 1ST POSITION

KEY OF G FLAT

G FLAT SCALE - 6TH POSITION

G FLAT ARPEGGIO - 6TH POSITION

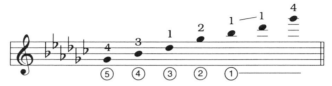

G FLAT STUDY #2 - 6TH POSITION

KEY OF G FLAT

G FLAT SCALE - 8TH POSITION

G FLAT ARPEGGIO - 8TH POSITION

G FLAT STUDY #3 - 8TH POSITION

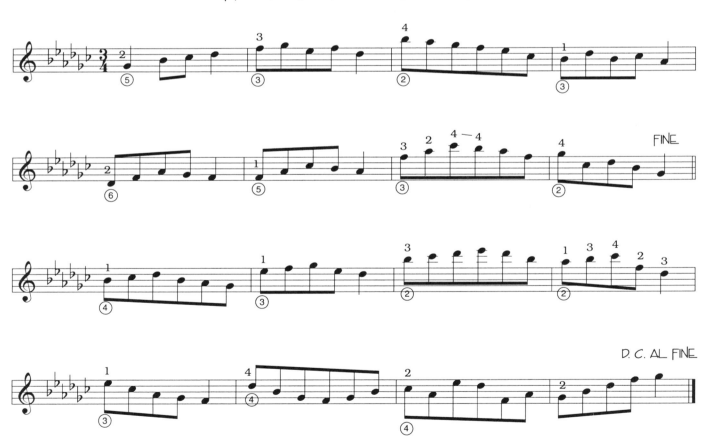

KEY OF G FLAT

G FLAT SCALE - 11TH POSITION

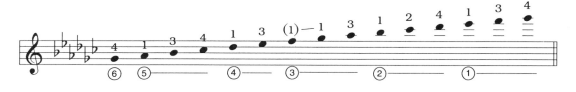

G FLAT ARPEGGIO - 11TH POSITION

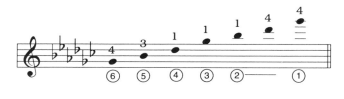

G FLAT STUDY #4 - 11TH POSITION

KEY OF E FLAT MINOR

E FLAT MINOR SCALE / HARMONIC MODE - THIRD POSITION

E FLAT MINOR ARPEGGIO - THIRD POSITION

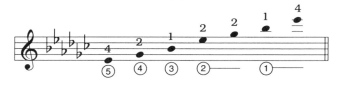

E FLAT MINOR STUDY #1 - THIRD POSITION

KEY OF E FLAT MINOR

E FLAT MINOR SCALE / HARMONIC MODE - 6TH POSITION

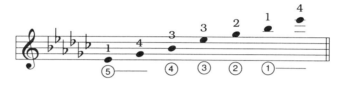

E FLAT MINOR ARPEGGIO - 6TH POSITION

E FLAT MINOR STUDY #2 - 6TH POSITION

KEY OF E FLAT MINOR

E FLAT MINOR SCALE / HARMONIC MODE - 8TH POSITION

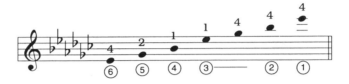

E FLAT MINOR ARPEGGIO - 8TH POSITION

E FLAT MINOR STUDY #3 - 8TH POSITION

KEY OF E FLAT MINOR

E FLAT MINOR SCALE / HARMONIC MODE - 11TH POSITION

E FLAT MINOR ARPEGGIO - 11TH POSITION

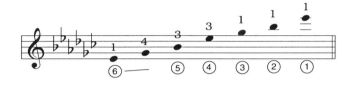

E FLAT MINOR STUDY #4 - 11TH POSITION

KEY OF C REVIEW

KEY OF A MINOR REVIEW

KEY OF G REVIEW

KEY OF E MINOR REVIEW

KEY OF D REVIEW

KEY OF B MINOR REVIEW

KEY OF A REVIEW

KEY OF F SHARP MINOR REVIEW

KEY OF E REVIEW

112

KEY OF C SHARP MINOR REVIEW

KEY OF B REVIEW

KEY OF G SHARP MINOR REVIEW

115

KEY OF F REVIEW

KEY OF D MINOR REVIEW

117

KEY OF B FLAT REVIEW

KEY OF G MINOR REVIEW

KEY OF E FLAT REVIEW

KEY OF C MINOR REVIEW

KEY OF A FLAT REVIEW

KEY OF F MINOR REVIEW

KEY OF D FLAT REVIEW

124

KEY OF B FLAT MINOR REVIEW

KEY OF G FLAT REVIEW

KEY OF E FLAT MINOR REVIEW

3RD POSITION

6TH POSITION

8TH POSITION

11TH POSITION

OTHER BOOKS IN THE SERIES

20896BCD - GUITAR JOURNALS BLUES

20905 - GUITAR JOURNALS CHORDS

20895BCD - GUITAR JOURNALS FINGERSTYLE

20925BCD - GUITAR JOURNALS FLAMENCO

20900 - GUITAR JOURNALS FLATPICKING

20897BCD - GUITAR JOURNALS JAZZ

20903 - GUITAR JOURNALS MASTERING THE GUITAR
FINGERBOARD: READING BOOK

20894BCD - GUITAR JOURNALS ROCK

20901 - GUITAR JOURNALS SACRED

20902 - GUITAR JOURNALS SCALE STUDIES

20904 - GUITAR JOURNALS TECHNIQUE